Idaho *Wildlife*

impressions

photography and text by **William H. Mullins**

FARCOUNTRY
PRESS

ISBN 13: 978-1-56037-413-8
ISBN 10: 1-56037-413-6

© 2007 by Farcountry Press
Photography © 2007 by William H. Mullins

For more information about our books, write Farcountry Press, P.O. Box 5630, Helena, MT 59604; call (800) 821-3874; or visit www.farcountrypress.com.

Created, produced, and designed in the United States.
Printed in China.

12   11   10   09   08   07   1   2   3   4   5   6

Front cover: During the fall rut, large bull Rocky Mountain elk tilt their heads back and bugle—a majestic sound that echoes across the landscape. These herd bulls gather cows into groups called harems—and spend much of their time driving younger bulls away.

Back cover: Tree swallows are noted for their steely, bluish green back and white throat and chest. Their favored habitat is open country near bodies of water.

Title page: These young burrowing owl chicks have ventured outside their nest, which is usually a six- to ten-foot-long tunnel. While burrowing owls are capable of doing some of their own digging, they often move into burrows vacated by badgers or other animals.

Right: Red foxes have expanded their range in recent years, and have come to inhabit cities and towns. This vixen and her young pup have a den at the end of a driveway in the town of Cascade.

Below: The willow patch in which this bull moose is bedded provides much of his diet during the winter. The moose is the largest member of the deer family and one of North America's largest land mammals.

INTRODUCTION

BY WILLIAM H. MULLINS

You can't choose your parents or where you're born, so I have always felt extremely lucky that I was born and raised in Idaho. What a great place to grow up and learn about the great outdoors!

The Clark's nutcracker is named after explorer William Clark of the Lewis and Clark Expedition. Its long, somewhat raspy call is a familiar sound in most of Idaho's coniferous forests. The bird is frequently spotted in its favorite perch, the tops of conifers.

The nation's thirteenth largest state, Idaho is nearly 500 miles long and just over 300 miles across at its widest point. Elevations range from 770 feet at Lewiston, where the Snake and Clearwater Rivers exit the state, to 12,662-foot Mount Borah in the Lost River Range in central Idaho.

While the state's mountains aren't as high as those in Colorado and elsewhere, they are certainly some of the most rugged terrain to be found anywhere on the continent—an opinion formed over many years of strenuous backpacking and elk hunting trips. I have always said (but cannot prove) that if Idaho was ironed flat, it would be larger than Texas!

Idaho boasts some of the deepest canyons in North America, including Hells Canyon, which defines the Idaho/ Oregon border; the Salmon River, which bisects the state into its northern and southern halves; and the 110-mile-long Middle Fork of the Salmon River.

The state's wide variety of habitat allows for an incredible diversity of wildlife. Idaho is home to 103 species of native mammals (plus 6 non-native species); approximately 229 species of breeding birds, with another 22 species or so that are regular migrants; 22 species of native reptiles; 13 species of native amphibians; and 68 species of native and introduced fish (40 are native and 28 are introduced).

Up north in the panhandle, the rainy, spruce-hemlock forests and ancient red cedar groves are reminiscent of the western Cascades and coastal ranges of Washington and Oregon. Grizzly bears, and even a few mountain caribou, roam the northern corners of the state.

Farther south, elk and white-tailed deer, black bears and cougars, songbirds and owls, and all sorts of other creatures inhabit these vast mountains, pristine creeks, and river canyons. In the distance, the buzzing "shraaaa" of a Clark's nutcracker floats through the trees. From a nearby Douglas fir, a brilliant indigo Steller's jay glides to the ground and hops about, looking for crumbs left from someone's sandwich.

On the upper Middle Fork of the Salmon River, a brilliant westslope cutthroat trout, the official state fish, rises from a deep, emerald pool to grab a size 14 Royal Humpy. After a few minutes, the fish is subdued, the barbless fly removed, and the fish is quickly released to fight another day. The spawning colors are spectacular: shades of greenish gold on its back, reddish orange along its belly, hints of copper and brass and a splash of purple on the head and gill cover, large black spots toward the tail, and of course that deep-crimson slash mark on the lower jaw that gives this beautiful fish its name!

In late spring, if you venture into the doghair stands of lodgepole pine that surround the jagged Sawtooth

Wilderness, you might come across a displaying spruce grouse, which looks like a miniature black-and-white turkey with a vivid crimson eye comb.

In Idaho's high country, bighorn sheep, elk, and mule deer make their living. Mountain goats can sometimes be spotted as tiny white specks high in the Sawtooth or Boulder Mountains; they pretty much have these steep, rocky escarpments to themselves. In the lower sage-studded hills of the Pahsimeroi, Lost River, Birch Creek, and other valleys, pronghorn race across the vast, open country. A golden eagle

Although grizzly bears used to range throughout most of Idaho, they are now found only in the Selkirk and Cabinet–Yaak Mountains in the far north as well as in eastern Idaho, adjacent to Yellowstone National Park. Their vision is about as good as a human's, but their sense of smell is believed to be about 1,000 times better than ours!

glides along a pine-studded ridge above the Middle Fork of the Salmon River, while below a blue grouse skulks along a stream bank filling up on hawthorn and serviceberries.

The Snake River has carved through a basalt and rhyolite canyon in the desert south of Boise, which forms the major geologic feature of the Snake River Birds of Prey National Conservation Area. The area hosts fifteen species of nesting raptors. In the spring, prairie falcons and red-tailed hawks resemble modern jet aircraft in combat as they engage in courtship flights above the canyon rim. On the canyon floor, long-eared owls are already feeding their young in thick willow patches, while a low-gliding northern harrier scouts a reed-choked island for a possible nest site. At night, courting Woodhouse's toads emit their eerie bawling courtship cries.

At dawn on the Owyhee Plateau in the southwest corner of the state, huge greater sage grouse males gather on breeding grounds called leks and strut around with huge white chests and pointed tail feathers, hoping to attract a female. The lek is replete with the hollow plop-dlop-dlop sound as the birds brush the leading edge of their wings against their inflated yellowish-gray esophageal air pouches as part of their unique courtship display. In the distance, coyotes bark and yip to each other across vast expanses of sagebrush.

Even the barren, rough-looking lava that flows in and around Craters of the Moon National Monument and Preserve hosts a variety of wildlife. Mule deer and elk winter in the area, and pronghorn graze in the open expanses. Tiny black-and-white striped yellow-pine chipmunks and golden-mantled ground squirrels delight many visitors with their antics.

At Grays Lake National Wildlife Refuge, the guttural, ancient call of greater sandhill cranes fill the morning air as flocks of black-headed Franklin's gulls leave their nesting territories to feed.

Above Henry's Lake in the northeastern corner of the state close to Yellowstone National Park, a lone grizzly bear watches two unsuspecting hikers on their way to fish in a high mountain lake in the Centennial Mountains.

The wild country and wildlife of Idaho shaped my life. My childhood was spent exploring the great outdoors, which led to my careers in biology and photography. I continue to love exploring and photographing the beautiful, rugged state of Idaho.

Populations of black-tailed jackrabbits are somewhat cyclic, reaching peak numbers approximately every six to ten years.

Lewis and Clark saw their first yellow-bellied marmot shortly after crossing Lemhi Pass into what is now the state of Idaho. Also known as rockchucks and whistle pigs, marmots are one of 45 rodent species found in Idaho.

Left: White-tailed deer are found primarily in northern Idaho, but their range is increasing elsewhere in the state, especially along riparian corridors.

Facing page: Three young ferruginous hawks (closely related to the red-tailed hawk) are silhouetted at sunset in the Snake River Birds of Prey National Conservation Area south of Boise.

Facing page: Until grey wolves were reintroduced into Idaho in the winters of 1995 and 1996, only a handful roamed the state's backcountry. Now, there are an estimated 650 wolves in 70 packs across the state. PHOTO BY DONALD M. JONES

Below: During winter, mule deer does, fawns, and young bucks tend to congregate in large herds on the winter range. Larger bucks often form their own groups during this time. These does and fawns are on their winter range near Boise.

Right: The familiar call of the Pacific tree frog is a harbinger of spring. These small green, tan, brown, or gray-colored frogs with distinctive black eye-stripes are found near just about any body of water.

Below: These kokanee salmon make their way up the North Fork of the Payette River north of McCall during fall spawning season. Kokanee and sockeye salmon are the same species, with kokanee remaining in landlocked lakes and streams and sockeye living in the ocean and breeding in freshwater. Both are silver with bluish-green backs in the summer but turn a brilliant crimson with olive green heads during spawning season.

Facing page: A hen ruddy duck guides her brood through the mirrorlike waters of a pond at Grays Lake National Wildlife Refuge in southeastern Idaho.

Above: America's second-largest rodent after the beaver, the porcupine is known for its sharp, barbed quills. The porcupine's diet consists almost entirely of woody plants, but it sometimes develops an appetite for things like the wiring, hoses, belts, and other vital components of vehicles left parked in the woods by hunters, hikers, and others.

Left: Muskrats are semi-aquatic, living either in burrows dug at the water's edge or in lodges made of cattails and other aquatic plants.

Right, above: One of more than fifty species of wood warblers in North America, this Nashville warbler is picking tiny insects from a blooming willow at the Nature Conservancy's Silver Creek Preserve in south-central Idaho.

Right and facing page: The call of the western meadowlark (right) is a short, sweet refrain, while that of the yellow-headed blackbird (facing page) sounds like the rusty hinge on a barn door.

Facing page: The pronghorn is the fastest mammal in North America, attaining speeds of nearly 60 miles per hour.

Below: Badgers dig numerous burrows for two reasons: to create homes for themselves and to locate prey, such as ground squirrels. Many animals, including coyotes and burrowing owls, take up residence in old badger holes.

A resident of mature pine and fir forests, this male blue grouse, with his inflated purplish neck sacs and raised yellow eye combs, is trying to attract a female during the spring breeding season.

The drake wood duck, one of Idaho's most striking waterfowl, is one of several duck species that nest in tree cavities.

Left: This mountain goat kid appears to be "smelling the roses"—or, in this case, a stalk of bear grass—in the Mallard-Larkins Pioneer Area in northern Idaho.

Below: A mule deer buck bedding down in a grassy meadow displays his velvety antlers. The velvet—which consists of thousands of blood vessels that deposit calcium and other minerals to the bony antler—is shed in late summer before the autumn mating season. Antlers can grow as much as a half-inch per day during mid-summer. In January and February, mule deer shed their antlers; then in early spring, they sprout a new set and start the process over again.

Right, above: Chukars are one of Idaho's most popular upland game birds. Native to Eurasia, chukars were introduced into Idaho in the 1940s. They thrive in arid, rocky canyons and hills in the southern and west-central portions of the state.

Right, below: A pair of American avocets are a study in symmetry on a small island in a pond in western Idaho.

Facing page: Black bear cubs are born without hair and are blind and helpless in mid-winter during hibernation. They emerge from their dens in spring and stick with their mothers for a year before heading out on their own.
PHOTO BY DONALD M. JONES

Facing page: When people find a mule deer fawn lying alone in the forest, they often incorrectly assume it has been abandoned by its mother. Deer leave their fawns in hiding places while they feed, returning regularly to feed and check on them. It is important to leave these fawns alone and not draw them to predators' attention.

Below: This young Rocky Mountain bighorn sheep ram is one of a large population living in Hells Canyon on the Idaho/Oregon border.

Facing page: Black-necked stilts and American avocets are closely related shorebirds that are frequently seen together in shallow ponds and marshes throughout southern Idaho.

Below: This black-crowned night heron gazes intently into a shallow backwater of the Boise River near Eagle waiting for a fish to swim by.

Left: Favorite foods of the grizzly bear include whitebark pine nuts and army cutworm moths, which hide under rocks during the day. Grizzlies can devour as many as 40,000 moths in a single day!

Below: Mountain lions, or cougars, have perhaps the largest historic range of any land mammal in the Western Hemisphere. At one time, they ranged from northern British Columbia to the southern tip of South America. Mule deer are their favorite prey, but they will eat a wide variety of animals, as well as some plants.

Facing page: The westslope cutthroat trout, one of four subspecies of cutthroat in Idaho, is native to river basins from the Salmon River north. It was declared Idaho's state fish in 1990.

Below: The mating call of the Woodhouse's toad, seen here along the Snake River in the Birds of Prey National Conservation Area, is an eerie, almost human bawling sound.

Below: A yellow-pine chipmunk nibbles a seed at Craters of the Moon National Monument and Preserve in southern Idaho. The yellow-pine chipmunk can be distinguished from its cousin, the golden-mantled ground squirrel, by its stripes; the chipmunk has stripes on both its head and its body, while the squirrel has stripes only on its body.

Above: During the fall, elk graze primarily on grasses and other non-woody plants. During winter months, they add woody shrubs to their diet.

Facing page: This western fence lizard blends in perfectly with a lichen-covered rock in the arid Owyhee Canyonlands in the southwestern corner of the state.

Above: Red-naped sapsuckers, such as this female perched on a juniper, are well named because they commonly drill rows of holes in tree trunks and lap the sap that oozes out. They also eat insects that get trapped in the sticky sap.

Right: This days-old American coot may be the original "ugly duckling," but its mom, at right, surely thinks otherwise.

Above: An adult ferruginous hawk feeds her four chicks, approximately fourteen to eighteen days old, in their nest above the Snake River in the Snake River Birds of Prey National Conservation Area.

Left: Rafters on the Middle Fork and Main Salmon Rivers in the Frank Church–River of No Return Wilderness in central Idaho often spot groups of Rocky Mountain bighorn sheep. Standing on the shore near the Middle Fork, this lamb glances back at its mother.

Left: Turkeys are not native to Idaho but have been successfully introduced throughout the state—to the delight of many hunters. If Benjamin Franklin had gotten his way, the turkey would be the national bird instead of the bald eagle.

Below: Chinese ring-necked pheasants, which were introduced into Idaho in the late 1800s, are another favorite with game hunters. Pheasants are found throughout the state—particularly in and near agricultural areas.

Facing page: The word "coyote" is believed to have originated with the Aztec Indian word coyotl, which means "singing dog" or "barking dog." Anyone who has heard these vocal creatures howling and barking to each other at night can understand how they've earned their name.

Left: One of three species of teal native to North America, the cinnamon teal is the only one with the namesake cinnamon color. It can be found throughout the state and is especially common in desert ponds, agricultural areas where there is water, and marshes.

Below: Terns are the graceful, svelte cousins of gulls. This Forster's tern sits on a floating nest made of bulrush stems in a marsh in eastern Idaho. Forster's terns capture fish by watching the water from a nearby perch, then diving in after their prey.

Right and far right: During the late-winter and early-spring breeding season, the male Columbian sharp-tailed grouse (right) and greater sage grouse (far right) gather on communal leks to strut their stuff in the hopes of attracting a mate. Their ritualistic displays include elaborate dancing, stomping, shaking, and noise-making.

Above: Mature bull elk commonly grow antlers with six tines, or points, as seen on this bull.

Facing page: During winter, cow, calf, and immature bull elk tend to occupy the central portion of their range, while mature bulls are usually found on the fringes. These elk were photographed in the Payette National Forest in south-central Idaho.

Right: There are six separate wild horse herds in Idaho, with a peak total population of about 800 horses.

Below: This still-downy golden eagle chick waits in its nest high on a cliff in the Snake River Birds of Prey National Conservation Area while its parents hunt in the nearby desert. The golden eagle is one of fifteen species of raptors that nest in this preserve.

Above: Whereas most owl species nest in cavities or stick nests in trees and hunt at night, the short-eared owl nests on the ground and frequently hunts for rodents in the daytime.

Left: This red fox is tending to her litter of five pups near her den in the foothills above Boise. The pups start coming out of the den when they are about ten weeks old.

Right, above: Cedar waxwings are so named because the tiny red feathers on the tops of their wings resemble drops of wax. One of their favorite foods is mountain ash berries.

Right, below: The eastern fox squirrel is an introduced species that has adapted to living in many of Idaho's cities and towns.

Facing page: A pair of California quail roosts in a lichen-encrusted sagebrush. The male has a black, question-mark-shaped plume on its forehead. The female's plume is smaller and straighter, and the markings on her head are not as striking.

Left: This hours-old Canada goose chick sticks close to one of its parents at the Fort Boise Wildlife Management Area in southwest Idaho. Some Canada geese have become urban dwellers—to the delight of some and the displeasure of others—and frequent parks and golf courses in many cities and towns.

Below: The beaver is Idaho's largest rodent. Adults can weigh between 22 and 75 pounds, and, unlike humans, beavers never stop growing. This beaver is eating willow bark on a stem like we would eat corn on the cob.

Right, above and below: The mallard is the most common duck in Idaho. The bright green iridescent head of the male is unmistakable.

Facing page: The recovery of the peregrine falcon is one of the greatest success stories of conservation, thanks in part to the efforts of the Peregrine Fund's World Center for Birds of Prey, located in Boise. Over a period of nearly thirty years, this group of dedicated people raised and released nearly 7,000 fledgling chicks across the continent in a successful effort to save this magnificent falcon from extinction. The peregrine was named the official state raptor in 2004, and an image of a peregrine graces the state quarter.

Left: These California bighorn rams in the Jack's Creek drainage in southwestern Idaho's Owyhee County are a subspecies of the Rocky Mountain bighorn sheep found elsewhere in the state. California bighorn sheep had disappeared from Idaho and surrounding areas by 1940 but were successfully reintroduced over a period of many years beginning in 1963. Interstate 84 across southern Idaho is considered the border between California bighorns to the south and Rocky Mountain bighorns to the north.

Below: A pronghorn doe casts a sideways glance as she makes her way across a prairie. Both male and female pronghorns grow horns, although the females' are smaller. Unlike antlers, which are shed annually, horns continue growing throughout the life of the animal.

Right: This juvenile northern saw-whet owl recently left its nest in a nearby tree cavity. The saw-whet owl has an asymmetrical skull and ear openings, with the opening on one side located higher than that on the other side. This asymmetry allows the owl to "focus" its hearing on both the vertical and horizontal axes, which enables the owl to locate prey with incredible accuracy, even on the darkest nights. Other birds and animals with symmetrical ears hear sound on only one axis.

Far right: Mallards nest nearly anywhere near water, from city parks and suburban backyards to ponds, lakes, streams, and marshes throughout the state. Chicks are born covered with a thick, insulating down and are walking, swimming, and feeding within a few hours of hatching.

Left: Mountain goats' feet are well-suited for steep, rocky slopes—their choice habitat. They are native to just four states (Idaho, Montana, Washington, and Alaska) but have been introduced to several others.

Far left: Early one September, this red squirrel, or pine squirrel, was seen carrying dozens of ponderosa pine cones to the edge of the Middle Fork of the Salmon River, where it deposited them in pools formed by large rocks near the river's edge. There were several large "rafts" of these cones. Red squirrels commonly place unopened pine cones in wet places. This prevents the cones from opening, and the seeds remain viable for years. Too bad the river will likely wash this squirrel's stash away before it gets to enjoy the fruits of its labor!

Right: These young ferruginous hawk chicks are probably within a week of fledging, or leaving their nest. The adult hawks construct stick nests in trees, on cliffs, on the ground, and sometimes on manmade nesting platforms.

Below: During the breeding season, the American white pelican develops a fibrous growth that looks like a small fin on top of its bill near the tip. This growth shrinks and is not visible during the rest of the year.

Left: Two- to three-year-old bull elk, such as this one, usually produce antlers (racks) with four to five tines, or points, on each side, rather than the six points seen in mature bulls.

Far left: The Canada lynx is a rare cousin of the bobcat and is equipped with large, furry paws that facilitate travel over snow. The snowshoe hare is its primary prey, and lynx populations tend to fluctuate with hare populations.

Right: Grays Lake National Wildlife Refuge, located in southeastern Idaho, is home of the largest nesting population of greater sandhill cranes in the world.

Below: Great blue herons display incredible patience. In a marsh or other shallow water, they will stand perfectly motionless for long periods of time, waiting for just the right opportunity to grab an unsuspecting fish or crawdad. In winter, they are often seen standing in open fields, where they prey on mice and voles.

Above: The mountain bluebird is the state bird of Idaho. Of the three species of bluebirds in the U.S., it is the only bluebird that does not have any rust color on its chest and sides, which makes it easy to distinguish from its local relative, the western bluebird.

Left: Black bears aren't always black; they can also be brown, cinnamon, or even blonde in color.

Below: The western, or prairie, rattlesnake is shy and not usually aggressive. There are no recorded deaths from a rattlesnake bite in the history of Idaho, but their bite can be quite painful, and immediate treatment is important.

Facing page: In winter, elk tend to congregate in large groups. Like domestic cattle, elk need to "chew their cud"—chew, regurgitate, and re-chew—as part of the digestion process.

Below: Even large mammals, like this mature Rocky Mountain bighorn sheep, may have a hard time surviving cold winters with deep snow. This ram is digging through the snow to find food. Males can have an especially tough time because they used up a lot of their fat reserves during the breeding season.

Right, above: This bushy-tailed woodrat peers out from his nest in a cave above Elk Bar on the Middle Fork of the Salmon River in the Frank Church– River of No Return Wilderness. Bushy-tailed woodrats are also known as packrats because of their propensity to gather shiny objects and stash them in or near their nests.

Right, below: The Piute ground squirrel, formerly known as Townsend's ground squirrel, is commonly seen north of the Snake River Canyon in the Snake River Birds of Prey National Conservation Area. In fact, the abundance of squirrels has helped the canyon's prairie falcons achieve the species' densest nesting population in the world.

Far right: It's early autumn, and this snowshoe hare is beginning to turn white around its feet. By winter, its coat will turn completely white to blend in with its snowy habitat.

Left: A Say's phoebe perches on the handle of an old hay knife before delivering this moth to her nest of four chicks. Say's phoebes belong to a group of birds known as tyrant flycatchers because they catch flying insects on the wing. They are most common in the deserts of southern Idaho.

Facing page: A mourning dove is raising her chick in a nest built in a planter hanging on the side of a house in Boise. This dove and her mate raised two broods in this nest one summer, while a pair in a nearby juniper raised three broods.

Right: Moose are expanding their range in Idaho, as evidenced by this cow feeding in a pond next to Highway 55, about 50 miles north of Boise—well outside traditional moose range. In years past, moose have been sighted in such unlikely places as a cornfield near Boise and the middle of the very sparse and arid Mountain Home Desert southeast of Boise.

Below: Even water birds take time for a nice bath, such as this drake mallard in a Boise pond.

William H. Mullins

William H. Mullins has been photographing Idaho's wildlife and landscapes for more than 35 years. A Boise native, he gained an early appreciation of the outdoors on the many hunting, fishing, and hiking trips he took with his dad. This interest eventually spawned a dual career as a wildlife biologist and nature photographer.

Bill's work has been published in numerous magazines, books, and calendars. He wrote a column on nature photography for *Idaho Wildlife Magazine* for 13 years, and his photographs appear in a Compass American Guide on Idaho. He has won numerous awards from the Outdoor Writers Association of America, Northwest Outdoor Writers Association, and the Idaho Press Club.

He lives in Boise with his wife, Colleen, and usually at least one black Labrador.

www.agpix.com/mullins

PHOTO BY BILL VIETH